MikWright . . . family style

other books by MikWright Ltd.

*happy birthday . . . blah, blah, blah*

*hey, girl!*

*your mother looks good . . .*

*who's your daddy?*

# MikWright . . . family style

tim and phyllis

MikWright Ltd.

**Andrews McMeel**
**Publishing**

Kansas City

01 02 03 04 05 TWP 10 9 8 7 6 5 4 3 2 1

ISBN 0-7407-1877-0

Library of Congress Control Number: 2001087370

---
### Attention: Schools and Businesses ---

Andrews McMeel books are available at quantity discounts
with bulk purchase for educational, business, or sales
promotional use. For information, please write to:
Special Sales Department, Andrews McMeel Publishing,
4520 Main Street, Kansas City, Missouri 64111.

we would like to dedicate *MikWright* . . . *family style*
to our many loyal fans. for nearly a decade, we've had
the good fortune to find a niche of readers who enjoy
our less-than-politically-correct humor.

thanks, merci, y gracias.

## acknowledgments

*MikWright . . . family style* brings together dozens of top-selling MikWright greeting cards in a format that begins to tell the near truth about the whole idea.

flagrant exaggerations and distorted facts begin to unfold as members of tim's, phyllis's, and bob's families are exposed for a greeting-card venture gone mad!

``what kind of mind buys this crap?" we ask.

at this time we wish to re-acknowledge our family members, friends, and business associates. by allowing us to lampoon your images, we are able to make our mortgage payments.

and to the many parties involved in our day-to-day operation, thank you for overlooking our oftentimes shoddy appearance.

we're trying to run a business for god's sake!

i ran into so many pricks that day
i thought i was at my family reunion.

actually, tim's family reunions were great!

his scandinavian grandparents bore twelve
young'uns so it was always crowded around
the three-bean salad and canned fruit medley.
thirty-five grandkids were a handful, to be sure.

they'd fish, swim, and sneak a beer while the
elders were gossiping about the new divorcée
in town and about how she had been seen at the
florence bar, puffing on a cigarette and wearing
too much lipstick. then the conversation
would switch to grain prices.

the investigation concluded,

there was seamen on the car.

don't be so naïve peggy. when marge was
talking about the other white meat,
she wasn't talking about pork.

i guess as much as they might have hated it,
our mothers would never complain. they would
buy it, prepare it, cook it, and clean the mess up.
and then, justly so, they would cut our fathers off.

we say, let the bastards bring home the bacon.

christmas is . . . by ronnie collins.

well, there was joseph and mary, and, then,
um, some reindeer flew off with three wise
guys, and the grinch stole jesus.

can i open my presents now?

you're kidding! i get both nipples?

nipples. what men don't seem to realize about nipples is that if they paid as much attention to their own as they do to others', they'd probably learn a whole new meaning to the word "yum."

the whole breast-feeding agenda has led to issues. for tim, imagine the horror when he found out that the other two siblings latched on, but he was the new-generation baby who got some sort of "milk replacer."

he still gets a pit in his stomach whenever he sees a woman breast-feeding her kid in public.

hello, bitter . . . party of one!

when fully erect . . . it would stop traffic.

you should see the stud that bucked me saturday night!

in retrospect,
earl should have married his
other cousin.

left to right . . . earl, melody, edna, and grady
(phyllis's in-laws, or some might argue, the out-laws).

no, they weren't going to a hee-haw audition, and
no, the roy clark look-alike contest wasn't in town.
it was church directory picture day.

up early to make sure everyone's outfits complemented
each other's, off to church they went.

we've all been there . . . the service and the
fellowship afterward with the minister's wife
bringing potato chips while everyone else
brought a baked chicken or green bean casserole
with durkee onions on top.

now edna sleeps in on sundays, watches televangelists for
kicks, and contributes to charities via the web.

for the life of me, i don't know
how i got that yeast infection.
i was in and out of that bakery
in less than a minute.

the competition at daytona was tight.
lucky for dorinda, judy misplaced
her thigh crème.

mildred, eunice, and elaine met last
saturday in downtown lancaster for lunch at
the chat and chew cafe. all hell broke loose
when elaine started choking on an asparagus tip.
mildred got her emergency procedures screwed up
and began mouth to mouth. well, you can imagine
the rumors that started.

you know the type . . . a little hankie tucked under
the watch, the slight aroma of b.o., and flakes
of dandruff the size of guppy food.

you can imagine the whole thing . . .
two caramel rolls for the three of them, one or two
cokes and a fifteen cent tip! "after all," one would
say, "they didn't tip me for cleaning bedpans for
twenty-three years!"

the chat and chew was fabulous.
unfortunately, it later closed when the salad bar
became trendy. technically, you didn't have to tip
at a salad bar.

who's gonna tell santa about prancer?

many scientists believe that the
brontosaurus could consume up to
3 tons of vegetation a day.

that's a lot of crap!

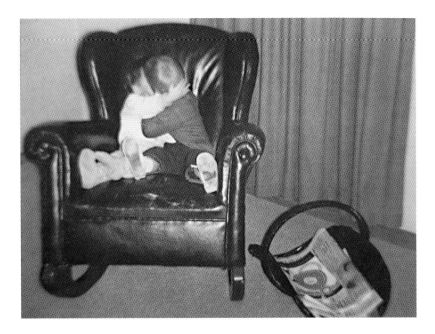

o.k., now that's enough boys!
we've got flowers to arrange.

tim always had a flair for floral arrangements.

he would pick bunches of wild flowers and mix them with dandelions for a beautiful centerpiece. of course, his mother half-raised an eyebrow, but since tim's brothers were out in the field, he needed something to occupy his time when he wasn't hanging laundry or making finger sandwiches.

can't you just imagine sitting next to "mouth"
on a greyhound bound for austin?

george always seemed to have a lot in common
with the ladies. often he would stop by
dottie's to gossip over brunch. then it was
straight back to the machine shop.
isn't that queer?

i was just three when i met my
uncle roy's roommate william.
dad still calls him "$3 bill."

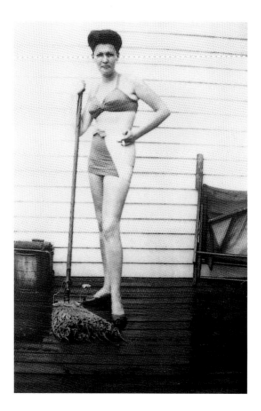

do i look like i give a rat's ass?

so who mops the deck in a trendy two-piece bathing suit
while dragging on a nonfiltered cigarette? why, aunt rene,
of course! with legs all the way up to her ass, you're
better off letting aunt rene do it her way.
(just ask any one of her thirty-four cats.)

hanging out in south florida these days, aunt rene
is content with a carton of cigs, a cheap bottle
of vodka, and a never-ending supply of olives.
you just want to squeeze the life out of her!

your mother sure knows how to
work a crowd.

mabel!

are you teaching that boy to cook?

what next . . . interpretive dance?

"ladies and gentlemen . . .
we'd like to welcome you to alabama.
please set your watches back six years."

tim remembers his first flight like it was yesterday. it was april 3, 1971, and his family flew from sioux falls to sioux city to kansas city to dallas. he knew then and there that he wanted to work for an airline.

his dad was fascinated with the stewardess's white boots and the complimentary peanuts. his mom was in pain. she had a calcium deposit on her knee, so she spent the entire vacation in bed.

once in dallas, they toured the g.m. plant where a glob of grease fell on tim's head. then, back at his uncle's ranch, a scorpion crawled into his pants and he screamed like a schoolgirl. next, a tree snake jumped into his cousin's dune buggy and again . . . schoolgirl scream.

tim's mom got better the day they left.

he recently spent fifteen years in the airline industry but now prefers to take his punishment with a yearly colon exam.

hi. my name is kevin. i am sad. my kitten is gone. mommy said he ran away. but, i think that's a bunch of shit and he got shot by that bastard next door.

get with it lenny!
when i said i needed a napkin
i wasn't talking about
a moist towelette!

"52" *Leona*

step right up . . . just 50 cents to see a
full moon in broad daylight!

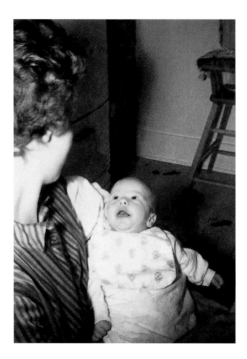

you're damn right i'm thirsty!
now which one of those things
makes cappuccino?

now we don't want to go on and on about the
breast-feeding thing, but here's our take on it . . .

some marketing genius decides that "pre-fab"
milk is the deal. did he or she ever once stop to
think about the plight of the world's children?
and what about the mothers?

bob was one of the boob castaways.
his issues are many. to this day he can't
properly suck on a straw!

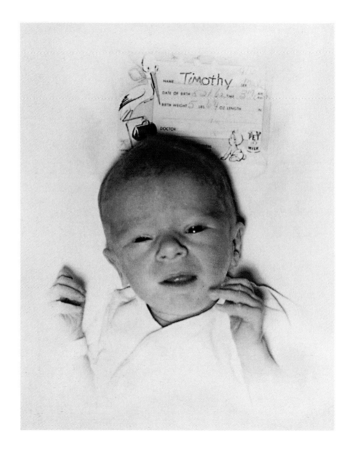

perhaps there was some truth to
dorothy's alien abduction story.

esther still stands a little funny as seen here
with her flowering bush. just last week she
said her hemorrhoids hurt her like a sore-ass
duck on a salt pond.

this was the house i grew up in. not much,
but it sure beats that piece of shit trailer park
you came from.

let's say this about that . . .
we don't have anything against trailer homes.

hell, phyllis was conceived up against a double wide.

. . . and then that bitch had the nerve to show up with jello instead of her assigned chicken casserole. now, i'm not one to gossip, but can you believe how fat she has gotten; bitch, please!

excuse me ma'am, we cannot leave the gate until you're seated . . . and from the looks of that ass, this flight is canceled!

yet another satisfied customer
from connie's cut and curl;
where they say . . .

"if your hair isn't becoming to you,
you should be coming to us."

"hello! jimmy hoffa . . . are you in there?"

to this day aunt mary complains of neck cramps, aerosol poisoning, and barrette syndrome associated with the '60s. the first one on the block to have a curling iron, aunt mary held it over everyone's head for years. then, with the advent of mousse, you'd have thought that she had bid within a hundred dollars and won both showcases!

so i called mavis to tell her i
got eight inches last night and,
of course, the bitch claimed she
got nine.

it was nearly impossible to tell the girls apart. fortunately, one picked left and the other picked right.

you didn't want to be around madge when it was
that time of the month. period. end of discussion.

ladies, i will not stand here and let you
talk about poor charlene like that, even
though we all know she gets more ass than a
toilet seat.

tim's dad's friend herman, or "cutty" as we called him,
had thousands of one-liners that usually ended with
a seedy little snicker. "more ass than a toilet seat"
was one of them. cutty used to work as an egg inspector
(eggs from chickens, not would-be mothers).

no longer with us, cutty and his first wife deloris
loved to sit in their pontiac on main street just
to watch the goings-on. later they would report on
sightings of the locals, perhaps dropping off a box
at the post office (what could it be?), or details
about a widowed teacher having coffee with
the banker (why?).

not ones to gossip, we all listened intently because,
of course, we were just as damn nosy as they were!

the gals were left alone whilst gary and
ronnie went to the boat show. they loved
their husbands . . . and everyone else's too,
for they were whores.

when emmett reached the peak,
he got off.

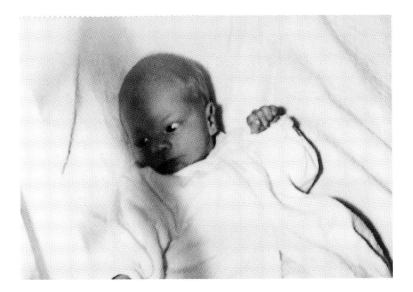

it was bad enough that the banker's son got
the part of jesus in the christmas pageant,
but the shit really hit the fan when they hung
a banner across the manger that read . . .
"jesus saves . . . at first national."

say no more.

so . . . we are at this "meet the author" gig in chicago and the sweetest elderly woman approaches us with tears in her eyes. she steps up and whispers . . . "is the boat in this picture the party boat from lake okaboji near spencer, iowa?" when we nodded yes, the tears streamed. "i grew up on that boat," she said. she explained how it later sunk but not her memories.

when tim's dad posed for this picture in 1952, he had no idea how many lives it would touch from vastly different walks of life. say no more.

he may have been a war hero
alright, but he never had the
guts to buy the old lady a box
of tampons.

finally, mr. right!

(or at least mr. right now)

everyone agreed, selma was the epitome of
trailer trash.

listen here you flat chested, broad assed,
penciled-in eye browed, tupperware snatchin'
wench! give me back my deviled egg carrier.

ah, the never-ending saga of tupperware.
surely you've been involved in a little tupperware
"lifting" of your own. you know, a friend drops off
a cake after your surgery, and you conveniently
forget to return the tupperware. uh, huh. time goes
on and it gets harder and harder to give it up.
you have no problem returning a cool whip container
or an aluminum pie tin, but "hell, no!
i'm not returning the tupperware!"

two words . . . kar ma.

i'll say one thing about ed . . .
when it comes to gas, he's always
got it.

o.k. then, it's settled.

a case of plutonium for a case of beer.

that leona was a looker
and the crown would have been hers, too;
if she had only said "world peace"
instead of "fashion first."

that leona, still a looker and still has that pale
yellow gown with black netting.

leona was a bit of a glamour-puss back then.
as a car-hop at the log cabin drive-in, she met
tim's dad the day he drove up in his swanky new
auto. (norman has to have a new car every three
years and waxes the damn thing at least once a week.)

wife, mother of three, grandmother of five, and
baker to the fortysome residents of the sunrise manor
nursing home, leona is the quintessential angel . . .
and can make one hell of a batch of aebleskivers!

some say that people look and even act like
their pets. well, now i can tell you that if
vivian lifts her leg . . . i'm gonna lose it.

kent is now eleven and still wets
the bed. danny turns eight in
january and is failing remedial
math class. timmy, our six year
old, only answers to "jessica."

i gotta tell ya. our cruise was great. we danced in the dominican republic, sang in san juan, golfed in guadaloupe, and got laid in lauderdale.

before . . . and after.

interesting thought, but no . . . vince is still vince and barbara is still barbara.

cousin vince, common-law husband, boyfriend . . . we don't know quite what to call him. he's been with cousin kathy for several years but we just can't seem to label the relationship. it's okay, though, we all like him and it makes for interesting chats when we've finished talking about the weather and the possibility of another crop disaster.

now barbara, she's got spunk! a true southern belle with that brasington gift for gab, phyllis's mother can charm the pants off you with one of her world-famous lemon pound cakes. with that never-met-a-stranger attitude, barbara floats through life as a friend to many and an angel to all. she's the best!

meet sven and olga, the original happy campers.

the right hand doesn't know what
the left hand is doing. if it did,
it would be jealous.

you don't have to yell!
obviously i can hear you.

now that i've got old lady kravitz'
house set on fire, it should be
about three minutes before those
big, strong firemen arrive.
do i look alright?

when you ask him he gets fidgety and quiet.
mr. williams has yet to explain why he was really
sitting on a fire hydrant. we can only surmise
that it involved small frogs, too much beer, and
a horse's head on the chancellor's desk.

we all have skeletons in our closets, or in
mr. williams's case . . . half of his frat brothers.

i've had it with that bastard!
i'm going home to mother!

you think that's bad . . .
i get one lousy tooth and the
bitch switches me to formula!

our next contestant
in the swimsuit competition
is mr. tennessee; herb odum.
herb enjoys hand puppets,
water aerobics, rabbit hunting,
and cross stitch.
herb was also voted this year's
mr. congeniality.

you know i'm not wearing any underwear.

although the visual may make you queasy,
we think regina was years ahead of her time.
a big-time bra burner, she's been breaking
barriers and busting glass ceilings from
maine to missouri.

perhaps most interesting . . . she used to be a man.

come on in!

i'm sorry, but robert's got diarrhea
and the kids both have lice, so . . .
it's just going to be us.

i hope you're hungry!

yes . . . grandma balked at first,
but we haven't seen a crow since.

stylish yet practical,
phyllis learned at an early age . . .
"you don't have to have a perm to
be beautiful."

lake norman was a wonderful spot to ponder the past and to "let" a silent killer if you so happened to be downwind.

what is it with gas, anyway?

america's fascination with "pull my finger"
and whoopee cushions is bizarre. it should be
the administration's top priority to worry less about
fluoride in the water and more about "bean-o" in
leafy vegetables.

our funniest true story about flatulence goes like this:

two guys are in a crowded elevator.
one slips a silent killer.
he steps out on the next floor,
turns to his friend and says "you common son-of-a-bitch."
doors close.

♪ ♪

    happy birthday to you,
      (you were a mistake)

    happy birthday to you,     ♪
      (the condom broke)

  happy birthday mary beth,
 (we can't afford to keep you)

    happy birthday to you.

i couldn't give a shit if i tried.

seven swans a swimming,
six geese a laying . . .
(make that 3 geese a laying)

don't look now, jeanette, but is
that her ass or did they raise
the titanic?

oh, they were polite, all right . . .
but, read between the lines:

"that dress looks so good on you, lorraine.
i like it more and more every time i see it!"

or

"you must be so happy for your children!
i think it's better for them when they're held
back a year, don't you?"

every year he would try out and
every year he would get cut.
finally he gave up cheerleading
and signed up for baseball.

it's a miracle she made it.
this is the girl who thought
asphalt was a rectal disorder.

hurry up and take the damn picture,
lillian! they're going to run out
of shrimp on the buffet!

let me say three words about your twig

on a card table . . .

white

trash

christmas.

one year it was a tumbleweed, the next a seedling,
and the next a failed ceramics-class creation,
and on and on.

it was the thought that counted. after all,
tim's family wasn't rich by any means, and perhaps it was
the precursor to his bizarre creativity. he was smart
enough to never have any neighbor kids over during
december (lest the entire grade school know about
his little "tree secret").

tim says . . . "get me through the holiday blues
so i can get on with my january depression."

you may see a man with two mules.
i see three jackasses.

not now mom, i'm a wreck. i've got a cake in
the oven, i'm supposed to meet sidney at the
ballet by eight, and i still haven't packed
for key west. now, for the last time mother . . .
i still don't have a girlfriend.

clark was handsome, no he was pretty. with that porcelain skin and kind nature and a flair for gourmet cooking; well, we all said a silent prayer for marlene.

timmy was only too happy to play the mommy.

it was a pivotal point in tim's childhood.

aunt marlene thought it would be "cute" to dress
him in his cousin karen's sailor outfit. he remembers
it like it was yesterday.

"it'll be fun," she said.

she was right.

what lesson did tim learn from this experience?

bring a cat to show-and-tell rather than spill your
guts about your weekend at aunt marlene's.

oh, and santa, i would also like a
pink dinette set, a u-bake-it
kitchen, and some white go-go boots
for my g.i. joe.

pardon me . . . just a little advice;

a shake for breakfast
a shake for lunch
and a sensible dinner.

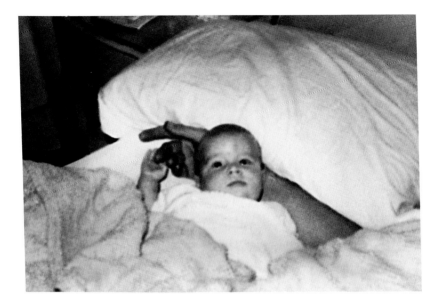

they tell me i used to lay in bed with
father's amputated arm to get me to go to
sleep. wasn't that sweet?

oh, come on, lighten up!

where tim comes from, if you factor in corn picker
accidents and animal attacks, a rural family of
eight would collectively yield seven. in truth,
only six of his nine uncles can count to ten
using their fingers.

keep sioux falls, just gimme that countryside.

cecil! you didn't use protection?

and just then jesus appeared and said . . .
"hey, kid, it's my birthday and that's
my puppy!"

what kid wouldn't be ecstatic over a new puppy?

well, tim paid for it the next year. although cloudy,
his recollection is painful.

he was opening the most beautifully wrapped, biggest box
under the tree, with "to: tim, from: santa," clearly
marked on the gift tag. it was the "billy blast off"
that he so desperately wanted. then the horror . . .

"oh my," from his mother's lips, "that is danny's gift.
santa must have put the wrong name on it." so . . .
he slid it danny's way wondering what pathetic sleeping
garment was somewhere under that tumbleweed of a
christmas tree. lucky him . . . tim got a chicken
that laid a ping-pong ball when the dart hit
it just right.

don't worry about him . . . he'll be fine.

while danny went on to become
an eagle scout, timmy went on
to date one.

your mother looks good, but
your father looks better.

big.          bigger.          just right.

did she have a mirror?

as an elementary school teacher, aunt kathy would line up
with the rest of the classroom on picture-taking day.
so, of course, year after year she developed quite
a collection of photos that sort of encapsulated
her look over time.

you must remember your mother rolling, teasing,
and curling for hours before some big night out
on the town. a little dippity-do, a few hours under
the hairdryer (with a cheap novel and a highball), .
and the world was hers.

you didn't hear it from us, but elvis lives! . . .
in aunt kathy's hair.

. . . in your wildest dreams!

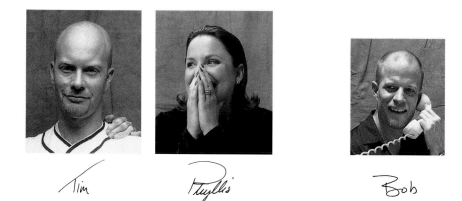

Tim        Phyllis        Bob

about the authors

although none of them would admit it, each secretly desires a
cameo appearance as an evil nursemaid *on all my children.*

if you get right down to it, tim and phyllis; not to mention
in-house creator bob, are stuck on stupid with just one friend . . .
prescription pain killers.

(sound familiar?)

who would have thought a farm kid and two military brats
would change "when you care enough to send the very best"

to:

"when you've got $3.25 to blow on a greeting card."